A Life With Significance

Leaving a Legacy Through Charitable Planned Giving

A Guide for Charities

Jim Van Houten

CLU, ChFC, MSFS, MSM

Cover Design by Chris Lilly.

Endorsements

The charitable gifting ideas Jim presented were game-changing for our nonprofit's major gifts and major donor engagement strategy.

Since the presentation, just a few months ago, we have secured over $500,000 (1/10 our annual goal) in major gift commitments by simply engaging some of our major donors in conversations about Charitable Remainder Trusts. We've also incorporated the tactics he's given us in our business donor cultivation strategies and have already secured $40,000 in commitments from business owners who are looking for creative win-win solutions to their corporate responsibility efforts.

> Brian D. Steele
> Executive Director
> Phoenix Dream Center

"A Life With Significance" provides professionals with the tips and techniques of charitable planning, how to recognize opportunities, and how to present complex strategies in a simple way to your own clients or donors. What sets this book apart is that you feel like Jim VanHouten is sitting right beside you, sharing his wisdom. Great information and a very enjoyable read!

> Cheryl Mott Smith
> Director of Gift Planning
> University of Arizona Foundation

Table of Contents

*Dedicated to Jon Fugler and Todd Isberner,
who inspired me to make this book a reality.*

"What man really fears is not so much
extinction, but extinction with
insignificance."

Ernest Becker
Pulitzer Prize winner

Introduction

Philosophers over the centuries have debated the motivations of man in desiring to help his fellow man. This help extends to our family, our community, our country and our world. This involves our time, our talents and our resources.

Most of us are so involved in earning a living that we do not think much about leaving a legacy. As we approach our maturity, we seek to leave something of significance so that we know that our lives mattered, that our being here made a difference to those who follow us.

Charities allow us to combine with others to make a greater impact than one person alone can do. Charities can hire staff to supplement and direct volunteers to do their important work.

We all cannot be Mother Theresa or Dr. Albert Schweitzer. However, we can make a significant impact by leaving a financial legacy to charity.

Part 1:
Planned Giving Overview

Ideas for Legacy Builders

We are blessed with many caring charities that are dedicated to improving the welfare of our world. The needs are great and resources are limited. Often the current donations are less than the budget needs. It would be a real blessing to any charity if there was a large endowment fund that would generate substantial cash every year for the charity.

We are familiar with the concept of giving to charity through cash, credit cards or checks. In addition, there are many other ways to give to charity. Some involve outright gifts, some are deferred gifts and some are split interest gifts. The following information will focus on unique ways of giving that may stimulate you to give, to give more or to give in a different way.

Life Insurance Cash Values as a Charitable Gift

Sometimes when a person reaches retirement or older, they may decide to cancel their cash value life insurance. The tax laws specify that upon surrender of the policy any amount of cash values that exceed the amount of premiums actually paid into the policy will be taxed at ordinary income tax rates. This could be a significant amount of taxable income on older, high interest earning policies. Alternatively, the owner could donate the policy to a charity and receive an income tax deduction for the value of the total cash values. The deduction will mean cash savings in your taxes. The charity can decide to surrender the policy and pay no taxes. The charity can decide to keep the policy in force and use the policy dividends to pay future premiums.

Deferred Gifts

These gifts are payable to charity at some date in the future. It may be at the death of the donor or it may be at a specified date in the future. Life Insurance is an ideal vehicle for a deferred gift. It pays the face amount of life insurance in cash at the death of the insured. Here are some examples of how life insurance can be used to leave a legacy with a charity.

Life Insurance to Create a Charitable Gift

To Leave a Greater Gift

There was a school teacher who really loved the Lord and her church. She was never married or had children. She was active in her church. Her only regret was that she did not have much to leave the church when she dies. To her it was important to leave a nice gift to the church. She learned that she could purchase a life insurance policy naming the church as the owner and beneficiary. In this way, a substantial gift would come to the church in her name. Since the church is the owner, the premiums are tax deductible. In fact, she would gift the premium to the church and they would pay the premium. She purchased a $ 100,000 policy. When she passed away, a check for over $ 100,000 was delivered to the church.

To Leave a Legacy at a University (or other charity)

One couple without children wanted to leave a legacy at their university. We asked the university about the cost to have a building named for them. The university required a $1,000,000 donation. They only had assets of $600,000 and that was not available until they died. We made an offer that would provide $1,200,000 to the university after their deaths. This would be 20% more than requested in cash now but would compensate the university for the delay in waiting for them to die. The university accepted the offer.

To secure the gift, the couple made the university the irrevocable beneficiary of their wills and they purchased a

$600,000 life insurance policy for the university. The building was named for the couple at a naming ceremony.

Life Insurance to Fund Multiple Charitable Gifts

In one instance a very successful businessman was lamenting the requests from friends for charitable donations. One time while we were visiting, he was interrupted by a phone call from one of his many friends asking for a donation for a charity. He stated to me that he is constantly solicited by friends to donate to various charities. He was frustrated by all this asking for cash. It was $2,000 here, $3,000 there. I asked if he would like to reduce this frustration.

"Yes," he said.

I set up a $500,000 life insurance policy for him. We listed one of his favorite charities as owner after they agreed to allow him to split up the beneficiaries as he directed. The next time he was asked for a charitable donation, he told his friend the following: "I will do something better. I will give the charity twice what you asked. However, they will have to wait until I die. I will add them as a beneficiary of a life insurance policy designated for charitable gifts." This led to numerous beneficiary designations on the policy.

His friends stopped asking so often. He like the idea so much that he took out another $500,000 life insurance policy when the first one was full. The premiums of these policies are tax deductible since he makes his checks out to the owner charity and the charity pays the premiums.

I personally have a similar policy with multiple charitable beneficiaries.

Officers and Directors Charitable Gift Plan

Sometimes employers can be useful in providing the means to make a sizeable gift to charity. One idea that can be used is the Officers and Directors Charitable Gift Plan. The donor, who is an officer or director of the company, has a desire to leave a substantial gift to charity upon his death. He purchases a very large cash value life insurance policy with the charity as beneficiary. The premium is paid by his employer, for which the employer has a lien against the policy and its cash values. Upon the donor's death, part of the proceeds is paid to the employer (equal to the premiums paid or the cash values, whichever is greater) and the balance of the proceeds is paid to the charity. The gift cost the employee nothing. This is a leveraged gift at its best.

Life Insurance to Replace Charitable Gifts

Sometimes donors are reticent to make large gifts to charity because they do not want to disinherit their heirs. Life insurance can be used to replace the gift with the life insurance proceeds. Life insurance proceeds can be paid out income tax free, gift tax free and estate tax free.

Stocks

Sometimes people have low basis, high value stocks. Selling them would mean long term capital gains taxes. Instead, these stocks can be gifted directly to charity. Then the charity sells the stocks and pays no taxes. The donor gets an income tax deduction for the value of the gift. The tax deduction means tax savings. In addition, the donor can do wealth replacement using life insurance. The donor purchases a life insurance policy equal to the donation. It pays off income tax free dollars to the donor's heirs upon the donor's death. This is especially significant with large charitable gifts.

Real Estate – Farm Land

Mrs. X wanted to make a multi-million-dollar gift to her deceased husband's favorite charity. She owned thousands of acres of farm land. None of her children wanted to be farmers. Selling the land would mean sales expenses, taxes, and commissions. So, she offered the charity a substantial portion of these acres. The charity made sure that there were not any environmental or legal issues with the land. Upon acceptance of this gift, Mrs. X received a substantial charitable tax deduction. The deduction was too large to take in one year (limit is 30% of adjusted gross income) so she was able to carry the remaining deductions forward for 5 more tax years. This meant substantial taxes saved.

Mrs. X then purchased a life insurance policy on her life owned by her children that equaled the value of the charitable gift. Upon her death, her children received the multi-million-dollar insurance benefit income tax free and estate tax free. This is wealth replacement at its best.

The charity later traded the land to a developer who had acquired some land that the charity could use for its expansion.

Real Estate - Undeveloped Land

In another situation, I met a developer who had a substantial tract of land on the corner of two major streets. His plan was to build a large apartment complex on the land. The neighbors who lived behind the project were very upset and vocal about the project. They were concerned about the noise and traffic this project would cause. They were fighting the developer in zoning hearings and threatening court actions.

I recommended that he consider donating nine acres of land to a charity as a buffer with the neighborhood. The charity could develop a community service facility there. The neighbors agreed and the developer made the donation of the land. He got a charitable deduction equal to the fair market value of the land.

The charity held the land for a few years. The apartment complex had all its entrances on the major streets and not into the neighborhood behind it. It turned out to be a senior oriented apartment complex and not noisy. The developer approached the charity with an offer to buy back the donated property. He purchased the land for the fair market value as determined by appraisers. This value was enhanced because of the apartment complex next door. He built more apartments on the land with no objections from the neighborhood. The charity ended up with over a million dollars that was used to build a community service facility a few miles away more centrally located to the community.

A couple of years later this same developer donated three acres of land in another city to the charity for the building of a community service center there.

Group Life Insurance as a Charitable Gift

Almost all top executives of major businesses get large amounts of group life insurance. These coverages can be as much as a million dollars. If the amount of coverage provided by the company is more than $50,000, then the cost of the excess coverage over $50,000 is added to the executive's W-2 income. Thus, the executive has to pay income taxes on this additional non-cash income.

One of my clients had $ 500,000 of executive group life insurance. I had asked him to consider a gift to a favorite charity of his. He consulted his CPA and then changed the beneficiary on $ 450,000 of excess group life insurance coverage to the charity. In so doing, he took a charitable deduction for the non-cash income he was charged. The result was a wash for tax purposes but a potential benefit for the charity.

Part Sale, Part Gift

Stock

The donor could use a part sale, part gift approach in selling an appreciated asset. The donor could gift part of the asset to a charity. Any income from the asset held by the charity would be income taxable to the charity, so no income or dividends should be paid. The purchaser of the asset would buy part outright from the owner and the other part from the charity. In this way, the tax savings from the income tax deduction on the charitable part can offset the tax on the sale part.

A 55-year old father is owner of a successful closely-held corporation. He has a son in the business and desires to have his son buy the business when he dies. He also has a strong desire to benefit a charity.

The solution:

- The father gifts $50,000 of the closely-held corporation stock to charity each year for 10 years. This saves him $20,000 in taxes each year.

- Parents gift tax-free $20,000 to the son each year.

- Son uses the $20,000 to buy and own $1,500,000 of life insurance on father

- Assuming death in 15 years and assuming the stock grows at 10% per year, son buys the stock from the charity for $1,500,000.

The son gets the business with a stepped-up basis. He gets the business without borrowing to buy it. The father gets to transfer the business to the son without income taxes, estate taxes, or gift taxes. He makes a substantial gift to charity.

Land

A church was interested in purchasing land for a new church building. They found 4 acres that met their needs. After negotiations, the seller and the church were thousands of dollars apart. The buyer did not want to budge and the church did not want to pay more. The church turned to a financial advisor for help.

The advisor suggested that the seller sell three acres for what the church wanted to pay and donate one acre to the church. The church would get the land for what it could afford. The seller would get a tax deduction for the donated land. The combination of cash from the land sale plus the taxes saved from the tax deduction of the donated acre would result in more cash to the seller than the seller had wanted originally for the four acres. This would be a win-win result.

Charitable Gift Annuity

This is where a donor gifts an asset to a charity in exchange for a fixed income for the rest of the donor's life. This is common in the charitable planned giving community. The donor may have a concern that the charity can meet its obligation for the next 20 or 30 years. The charity must maintain reserves to make sure that it will meet its obligation.

There was a donor who wanted to donate a large parcel of land in a valuable area of town in exchange for a gift annuity. The appraisal of the property was done and the calculations were made of the amount of income stream to be paid to the donor. Then the charity went to various insurance companies asking for bids for providing this level of annuity income.

Several bids came in at a cost less than the value of the land. The charity accepted the land and began making payments to the donor. Shortly thereafter the charity sold the property for the appraised value. They took part of the proceeds and bought an annuity from an insurance company that guaranteed the income to the donor.

The donor was now assured that a large life insurance company would be paying the life income stream. The charity was relieved of the obligation and kept the difference between the sale price of the property and the cost of the annuity. The difference happened to be over $100,000.

The Last Tithe

In the Bible, there are numerous references to giving to the Lord 1/10 of the first fruits of our labors. Many people strive to give a tithe to charities each year. A tithe is 10% of income. In our personal wills and trust, we put in **The Last Tithe**. Upon our deaths, 10% of all we own upon our deaths will go to The Last Tithe. In The Last Tithe section of our trust, we have listed which charities will share in this amount.

Split Interest Gifts

Split-interest gifts can be used when a donor is not willing or able to contribute the asset to charity now. In a split-interest gift, both the donor and the charity can benefit.

All such plans generate a current income tax deduction. Some plans will pay the donor an income for life with the assets passing to charity upon the deaths of the donors. Some plans provide an income to charity for a specified time period with the assets passing to the donors or heirs after the time period expires. They all benefit charity.

Charitable Remainder Trust

A very effective method of giving is the popular Charitable Remainder Trust. A charitable remainder trust (CRT) is a split interest vehicle. It provides current benefits to the donor and ultimate benefits to charity It provides an income stream for life or for a term of years. When the term ends or the donors die, the assets of the CRT pass on to the selected charities. The gift to the CRT generates a partial income tax deduction (usually 30-40% of the value of the gift). A CRT is an irrevocable trust.

The donors control the CRT, including making all the investment decisions. The sale of appreciated assets in the CRT avoids any capital gains taxes. CRTs offer the following benefits:

- Annual income for the donors

- Immediate income tax charitable deduction

- Elimination of capital gains taxes on sale of appreciated property

- Estate tax savings

Donors are usually concerned about disinheriting their heirs by gifting to a CRT. This concern is handled by purchasing a like amount of life insurance in a wealth replacement trust. The premium is covered by some of the income from the CRT.

The donor creates a charitable remainder trust with the donor as trustee. He then gifts assets to the trust. The trust provides that a specified percentage of assets must be paid to the donor each year. Upon the donor's death, the assets are transferred to charity. There is a calculation dictated by government rules that is done in setting this up. The calculation determines that using prescribed interest rates and life expectancy the charity can reasonably expect to receive no less than 10% of the original assets. The calculation determines the amount of tax deduction the donor will get.

The higher the payout percentage, the lower the tax deduction. The older the donor, the higher the tax deduction. The CRT is a tax-sheltered vehicle that does not incur income taxes on its transactions.

For example, a donor couple age 75 funds a CRT with $1,000,000 of low basis, high value assets. The payout rate is 8% of the asset value for the previous December 31. The calculated charitable deduction is $330,000. The CRT can sell the assets without incurring taxes. The donor couple will receive 8% of the assets remaining in the trust until they both die. The charity will receive what is left over after the deaths. The assets used can be stocks, bonds, real estate and even business interests.

Stock

There was a nice widow who was at that time age 76. She had $ 800,000 of Chase stock that she had held for more than 30 years. Her basis was very low. The stock was paying a 1.5% dividend. That is $12,000 a year income for her. She was recommended to use a CRT to increase her income. Here is how it worked. She placed the Chase stock in the CRT and avoided $150,000 in capital gains taxes. The CRT payout rate was 10%, which was a substantial increase in her income. Her first-year income was $80,000. She received an income tax deduction of more than $ 320,000. This resulted in cash savings of more than $81,000 in taxes. She then took 20% of this new income to purchase a life insurance policy for $800,000 for the benefit of her heirs.

Real Estate Lot Next Door

I was introduced to an inner-city charity that really wanted to acquire the lot next door. It would allow them to add more programs for the inner-city youth they are serving. The business owner was retiring and had the property for sale. The problem was funding the purchase. To pay for the lot, the charity would need to pay installment payments over a 15-year period plus interest on the loan. This was out of their reach. A member of their Board approached me to come up with an idea to make the sale happen.

I spoke to the business owner about the consequences of selling the property. We discussed the potential taxes on the sale, what he would do with the proceeds, his overall retirement income need and sources. We also discussed how much he liked the charity next door and that he would like to help them.

The plan developed called for the business owner to transfer the business to a CRT which would immediately sell the business to the charity for an interest only note at the interest rate of 8% per year. The note would be due and payable upon the deaths of the business owner and his wife. The CRT would pay out 8% per year to the business owner and his wife for life.

This generated an income tax deduction of over $300,000 which meant a tax savings of over $75,000. Of the income generated by the CRT, they used 2% to buy a life insurance policy equal to the value of the lot sold. The heirs will get the full value of the lot when the business owner and his wife die.

The interest only payment at 8% was considerably less than

the payment of interest and principal would have been. Here is the real blessing. The charitable beneficiary of the CRT was the charity next door. Upon the deaths of the business owner and his wife, the charity will get their own interest only promissory note back. They can rip up their own note.

My Parents' Experience

My parents had three sons. In their estate plan, they divided their estate into four parts: one for each son and one for charity. I visited with my parents and suggested that they use a CRT instead of dividing their estate four ways.

After reviewing the idea with their CPA, they set up a CRT funded with a fourth of their assets. They were both in their mid-80s at the time. The CRT was set up to pay out 10% of the assets as an income to my parents. My parents got a tax deduction that was substantial and taken over four tax years.

My mother died three months after setting up the CRT. My father lived for ten and a half years longer. In that amount of time, he received almost as much income as he originally contributed to the CRT. He gave the annual income from the CRT to charities.

Through careful management of the CRT assets, there were assets remaining in the CRT after my father's death to pay out 70% of the original amount contributed to the CRT. Between the annual income donations to the charities and the final payout, charities received much more than getting one fourth of the final estate.

My father received substantial tax savings of more than $41,000 and the CRT funded his charitable gifts for over 10 years. He left plenty of life insurance for his heirs to cover the value of the charitable gift.

As Deferred Compensation

In a discussion with the CEO of a large hospital, he was offered a $20,000 raise however he was concerned that taxes would take $ 8,000 of the raise. He did not need the money now but would like it to be available for retirement.

It was recommended that the CEO set up a CRT. The CEO contributed the $20,000 each year to the CRT. His income tax deduction the first year was $6,000. It increased each year thereafter. He paid the taxes on the $14,000 difference above the deduction. He also bought a life insurance policy to cover the value of the funds in the CRT.

He used a special type of CRT known as a Net Income with Make Up Provision Charitable Remainder Trust (NIMCRUT). This is like a CRT except that the donor can choose when to take an income. The donor can also catch up on prior payments not taken. This stop and go opportunity allows the donor to defer the taxability of payments to some future time. The only disadvantage is that if the donor dies before catching up on deferred payments, those remaining payments are given to the charity. One idea is to have the NIMCRUT purchase life insurance policies on the donors so that upon the death of one donor, the survivor donor will have even more assets to live on.

The NIMCRUT must use an annuity as its investment vehicle. Otherwise, when any other investment vehicle generated income or capital gains, the donors must take an income and catch up prior years.

When the CEO retired, he started a stream of income from the annuity. Upon his death, the remaining balance in the annuity will paid to the designated beneficiary. In this case, the charitable beneficiary of the CRT is the hospital where the CEO worked. Some of that bonus will come back to the hospital.

Charitable Lead Trust

The opposite of a CRT is the Charitable Lead Trust. A Charitable Lead Trust (CLT) provides a gift of income to a charity for a period of time. At the end of the period of time, the remaining assets in the CLT either return to the donor or pass to non-charitable beneficiaries (like heirs).

A CLT is an irrevocable trust. In a CLT, you set up annual contributions to charities from the trust for a fixed term. After the term, the remaining assets in the trust will go to you or to your heirs. A CRT works in reverse - you or your heirs will receive payments from the trust and the remainder will go to charity after a fixed term or death.

The Building Fund Gift

In one situation, the charity asked a wealthy donor for a donation for a building campaign. He gave them $5,000. They were expecting him to give $50,000. They did not want to appear ungrateful by asking him for more.

In an interview with a financial advisor, he disclosed that he was thinking of retiring in 10 years and did not want to give away money until he knew that he had enough money to retire. He was asked if the charity could "borrow" some assets for ten years. He said that he had $ 500,000 that he could loan them if he could get it back in ten years. The cost to him of that gift would be the lost interest he earned on the money in the bank minus income taxes he would have paid. This cost was about $6,000 a year. That was acceptable to him.

The CLT invested the funds in quality 10-year bonds that paid 7% interest which was equal to $35,000 a year in interest. The charity then borrowed $300,000 from a mortgage company on a 10-year mortgage to help build the building. The mortgage payment was entirely covered by the interest from the bonds. At the end of ten years, the mortgage was paid off and the assets in the CLT were returned to the donor.

Originally the charity received a $5,000 gift from the donor. They had hoped for $50,000. They actually received $300,000.

Jackie O Trust

The CLT may be useful in transferring appreciating assets to heirs with little or no gift or estate taxes. Jacqueline Kennedy Onassis and the Walton family were big users of CLTs. The Walton family (of Walmart fame) have billions of dollars in CLTs. Sometimes CLTs are referred to as Jackie O trusts.

Jackie O put her $50,000,000 estate into CLTs that lasted 24 years. Transferring the assets resulted in sizeable estate taxes which were offset by the present value of the income stream paid to charity over the 24 years. These assets appreciated over time, so she was able to transfer substantial assets to her heirs with very minimal taxes.

Terminally Ill Donor

One terminally ill donor put his assets into five CLTs that varied as to payout percentage and term. The results were that the children inherited part of the estate every five years for twenty years and reduced the estate taxes from $5 million to less than $1 million.

How It Works Best

Most donors structure charitable lead trusts so that the estimated value of the reportable gift which is also the remaining assets for distribution to beneficiaries is zero or close to it. Remember that the IRS will calculate the remaining value in the trust when it was established. Even if the trust's value appreciated considerably during its term, the income from the trust can still escape transfer and estate taxes.

To be beneficial to the heirs, the trust's rate of return should beat the applicable federal rate (AFR) assumed interest rate at the time of establishing the trust. If like the Walton family, your trust assets grow at 14% per year and the AFR when you established the trust was 3.4%, you will be earning more than you are giving to charities. When the term ends, the beneficiaries will receive the remaining trust assets tax-free.

In Summary

These charitable planned giving ideas and many more like them are available to help you leave a legacy that gives lasting significance to your life. As you have read, there are ideas for those with modest estates and those with substantial assets.

If something herein has stimulated some questions or interest, please talk to the person who gave you this book. Resources are available to provide answers or design a plan that is customized for you.

None of us has a guarantee of how long we have left to live. The time to begin building your lasting legacy is now while you still can. Make yours **A Life with Significance**!

Building the Bridge for Him

An old man, going on a lone highway
Came at the evening, cold and gray,
To a chasm, vast and deep and wide,
Through which was flowing a sullen tide.
The old man crossed in the twilight dim
That sullen stream had no fears for him;
But he turned, when he reached the other side,
And built a bridge to span the tide.

"Old man," asked a fellow pilgrim near,
"You are wasting strength in building here.
Your journey will end with the ending day;
You will never again must pass this way.
You have crossed the chasm deep and wide,
Why build you a bridge at the eventide?"

The builder lifted his old gray head.
"Good friend, in the path I have come," he said,
"There followeth after me today
A youth whose feet must pass this way.
This chasm that has been naught to me
To that fair-haired youth may a pitfall be.
He, too, must cross in the twilight dim;
Good friend I am building the bridge for him."

Will Allen Drongoole

Section 2:

A Handbook for Charitable Planned Giving Ideas

The purpose of this section is to prepare you to market the charitable planned giving ideas described in the first section.

I was briefly involved with a charity in California that in 10 years had increased their endowment fund from under $500,000 to over $20 million. During that period, they focused attention on learning about planned giving ideas. As they made current giving requests, they looked for opportunities to present planned giving ideas as well. They educated their Board, staff and volunteers about these ideas and the type of people to approach. Then they approached selected potential donors using some of the ideas described in this book. The results were an overwhelming success.

What is Planned Giving?

Planned giving is the art and science of making charitable gifts that are designed so that the donors can enjoy the benefits of the intended gift during their lifetime. These may involve wills and trusts, life insurance, or split-interest gifts.

Split-interest gifts are used when an estate owner is not willing or able to contribute the entire asset to charity during his lifetime. In a split-interest gift, both the donor and the charity benefit.

All such plans generate a current income tax deduction that save the donors income taxes. Some plans will pay the donor an income for life. They all benefit charity.

Why seek Planned Giving gifts when the money is needed now? Will Planned Giving reduce current giving?

Most charities have a need for more cash to carry out their missions. Their focus is primarily on raising cash now. Many resist any planned giving activities out of fear that they will lose focus on current fund raising.

How much easier would life be for the charity if a substantial portion of their annual budget was provided by their endowment fund? The need for today's fund raising would be less if planned giving had been done years before. Planned giving creates alternate sources of income and principal.

Planned giving opens up donors that may be closed to current giving. Some plans can actually generate some cash now for charities.

Experience has shown that current giving does not diminish when a charity actively promotes planned giving. Donors realize that the charity has ongoing current needs. With planned giving, they see an opportunity to leave a legacy for the charity. Experience has shown that once the donors commit to a planned gift, they will focus more of their annual gifts to those charities where they decided to leave a legacy. The charity will have tied the donor closer to itself.

Know about Taxes

Most donors are motivated in part or whole by tax savings. It helps a lot if the charity's representatives understand the income, capital gains, gift and estate tax rules. One key point to remember is that the deductions for charitable gifts are limited to: 50% of Adjusted Gross Income (AGI) if cash is given; 30% of Adjusted Gross Income if property is given.

You could have a combination of 30% of AGI in property gifts and the balance up to 50% in cash. Any charitable deduction in excess of these limits can be carried forward for up to 5 tax years.

Successful people look for ways to save taxes.

"Sometimes you can make more money by saving taxes than by making more money."

Resources

There are some excellent resources available to educate and train you in these planned giving ideas. You may want to research on the internet these subjects. It is recommended that you consider additional training at schools and seminars offered by the leaders in this field. Here are two such leaders in this field.

Crescendo: They offer marketing, software, training and administration support. Their software is excellent. It allows you to calculate and demonstrate CRTs, CLTs and gift annuities to potential donors. They have excellent articles and reference material for your use. Their website is www.crescendointeractive.com. Their phone number is 800-858-9154.

Pentera: They offer marketing, training, and support materials. They have excellent marketing materials and training, as well as seminars and training sessions all over the country. Their website is www.pentera.com. Their phone number is 317-875-0910.

Planned Giving Academy: They offer articles on various planned giving ideas by specialists in this field. In addition, there is a directory of planned giving specialists across the country. These include attorneys, CPAs, insurance professionals and investment advisors. Their website is www.plannedgivingacademy.com.

You may want to find a CLU, CPA, and CFP who has expertise in charitable planned giving. Actual experience, knowledge and ethics is very important.

Marketing – Sharing the Word

First you must understand the Psychological Pyramid of Priorities that wealthy people have. The pyramid is this:

1st Priority   Take care of themselves

How much is enough for us?

2nd Priority   Take care of their children or heirs

How much is enough for our heirs?

3rd Priority   Take care of others

Until families determine how much they need and how much their heirs need, they will always give less than they can or maybe even should. It shows understanding and compassion when you seek to help them get the answers to these priorities. It will also allow them to be as generous as they want. Sometimes you can utilize a life insurance professional (CLU) or financial advisor (CFP) to help the potential donor to quantify these priorities.

How Do We Find Wealthy Potential Donors?

The key word is wealthy, not potential donor. Many people do not realize that they are potential donors until they see the

possibilities of a win-win relationship with your charity. With the tax saving charitable planned giving ideas you have available, you can turn the wealthy into donors.

You are going to probe for information that can lead to a planned giving opportunity. You are also going to educate them on the various opportunities that exist for donors. Initially you will not know which idea will appeal to them so you should mention all of them in the hope that you touch a "hot button" with them.

Start with the Board and Staff

Educate your Board on these ideas and opportunities. Have them read these Charitable Planned Giving Ideas outlined above in A Life with Significance. They may be candidates for some of these ideas. They may be additional eyes and ears to look for potential donors who could benefit from these ideas. Are there any Board members for whom one of the ideas may be appealing? Do they know some people who might want to learn more about these ideas? Do they know donors who have a high potential to give? Do they know persons with high value, low basis assets that they may want to sell? You can save them taxes. Will they introduce you to them?

Present Donor Base

Look at your present donor base. Where do they live? Certain areas of your town attract the wealthy. Are any of your donors wealthy? Like elephants, the wealthy run in herds. If your goal is to find elephants, follow one to the herd. Ask your donors to invite you to some of their social functions. Your goal is to meet people and then follow up later. Ask your wealthy donors to introduce you to wealthy people that they know.

Meet with Community Leaders

Community leaders may be wealthy. They will know who is wealthy. Educate these leaders about your mission and place in society. Tell them how you want to approach the wealthy to make them aware of the win-win possibilities of planned giving ideas.

Educate Advisors

Meet with a few attorneys, CPAs, CLUs and CFPs who seem to be well connected to the wealthy to educate about your mission. Review with them the possible ways that wealthy clients can benefit from planned giving ideas. Emphasize the ability to save taxes.

These advisors could be your planned giving advisory board. They will like cross referral possibilities. The idea of planned giving gives the advisors new ways to better serve their clients.

You should look for those who are well established in their fields with good reputations, successful and still aggressive in business style. A professional who is coasting in his career can ruin your board.

Contact Retired Business People

Contact retired business owners, executives, or business leaders. As they get older, they tend to get more concerned

about the future of their communities and the youth. They want good values to be perpetuated. They want to support those charities that meet these needs. However, they are also very concerned about not outliving their resources or disinheriting their heirs. Your planned giving ideas can alleviate their concerns and meet their needs.

Charity Balls and Golf Outings

Look at the names of people who attend local charity balls and golf outings. Often a picture identifying them is published in the newspaper. These people are donors of current cash to charity. Perhaps you can make them planned givers as well.

Special Social Function

Consider a special social function for your planned givers and board officers. At that function give them an update of your progress toward building a planned giving base. Give them an overview of planned giving ideas. Perhaps you can give them a copy of **A Life with Significance**.

Ask them for help in identifying others to approach. Have them schedule appointments for you.

Other Marketing Ideas

Read the newspapers and local business journals for stories about successful business owners. Seek support from luxury automobile dealers. They cater to the wealthy. Try to get the dealers on your board. Approach business brokers. They know what business owners are selling their businesses.

These people will soon have a lot of cash. You may even be able to help them make the sale happen by showing the seller how to save money on taxes. In one large business sale, the seller agreed to the lower price offered by the buyer because a CRT was used to reduce the taxes thus saving the seller cash.

One Caution

Do not underestimate a person's potential. If you read the book, "The Millionaire Next Door," you will find that many multi-millionaires lead simple, not flashy lives. Their potential for giving is often greater than those who spend a lot to keep up appearances.

There was a couple in Albuquerque, NM who lived in a modest house worth about $200,000. The wife drove an older model Cadillac and the husband drove an older model Chevy truck. When interviewed, it turned out that the couple was worth $20 million dollars. You just never know.

"Whoever multiplies his wealth by interest and profit gathers it for him who is generous to the poor."

Proverbs 28:8

How to Approach the Wealthy. What do I say?

There are no "magic" words. However, there are some phrases or concepts that may get their attention.

In person:

- "Are you paying more taxes than you would like?"

- "How would you like to disinherit the IRS? When you and your spouse die, the IRS levies a tax on all your assets before they pass to your heirs. There are some exemption amounts allowed. If your estate is subject to tax, we may have some ideas on how to reduce the taxes."

- "Do you have an asset high in value, low in basis that you would like to sell someday? We have ideas on how to reduce the impact of taxes."

- "Have you ever seen the Psychological Pyramid of Priorities?" (show and explain the chart) "Is this true in your case? Have you quantified what is needed in Priority #1 and how much is needed for #2? We have ways of helping you analyze these priorities. May we help you?"

- "Are you a philanthropist? Involuntary (taxes) or voluntary (charity)? We have ideas on how to turn your involuntary philanthropy into voluntary philanthropy."

- "May I show you some charitable tax planning ideas that other wealthy people have found of real value to them?"

- "Have you ever heard of a charitable remainder trust or charitable lead trust? Would you like to know more about how these vehicles can reduce your taxes and enhance your wealth?"

- "If I could show you a way to reduce your taxes now, enhance your financial situation, and leave a legacy for your community, will you give me an hour of your time?"

- "I have heard and read nice things about you. You have certainly achieved a lot. Have you given thought to what kind of lasting legacy you want to leave in this community?"

- "An author once wrote: "What man fears most is not extinction but extinction with insignificance." How do you feel about that statement? A person can make a lasting impact on their family, business and community. I have some ideas that I would like to share with you about ways that you can make a lasting impact on your community."

On the phone:

- "If I promise not to ask you for a donation, will you meet with me to explore some win-win ways we can help you with your taxes and ways you can help us with our mission?"

- "How would you like to disinherit the IRS? Sometimes you can make more money by saving taxes than you can by making more money. May I have an hour of your time to explore some

charitable tax ideas that other successful people
have utilized to save taxes?"

- "Thank you for taking my call. You may be aware
  that I have an expertise in charitable tax planning.
  This means reducing taxes and giving to your
  favorite charities instead of the IRS. Would you
  like to have a choice where your tax dollars go?
  Let's get together for an hour so we can explore
  your options."

- "I need your help in developing ways to approach
  successful people like you with some creative
  charitable tax programs. Your knowledge,
  wisdom and guidance would be valuable to me.
  May I have some of your time next week on
  Tuesday or is Thursday better?"

In your approaches on the phone and in person, it is
important to know what you are going to say. You should
appear comfortable, smooth and confident. This comes from
developing your own scripts, memorizing them and then
practice. Your scripts need to be personalized to you, honest
and professional.

A professional actor recites the words as if they were
spontaneous, never giving you pause to think that the words
are memorized, and yet you know logically that they were.
You need to be a bit of a professional actor, know what you
intend to say without stumbling. The only way to do this is
through memorizing and practice.

Among the approaches given to you, find those that are most
comfortable to you. If you want, you can modify the words.
Write out your approach and memorize it. Practice on your

associates and friends. Do it enough that you find the words just seem to flow to you without you realizing it. Now you are ready for potential donors.

In this field, **ad lib is for amateurs**. Be prepared.

Objections

You may face some objections. If you do, then you may want to consider these responses.

Your prospective donor says: *"I have my tax specialist, CPA, etc. to keep me abreast of tax saving ideas."*

- "All of our wealthy donors have competent tax advisors. My role is to bring to you ideas in the area of charitable tax planning. The world of taxes is very complex. We find that few tax advisors ever focus on charitable tax planning. Any ideas we bring to you will obviously be reviewed by your tax advisor. I am sure he or she will not mind us giving you some new ideas."

- "That is good. As we discuss various charitable tax savings vehicles, we will need your tax advisor's input. Do you want him or her to join us at our first meeting?"

Note: our experience has shown that very few advisors know enough about charitable tax saving strategies. They have heard something about them but do not have detailed knowledge or personal experience in this area. They can be your allies if you educate them and make them feel a part of the team.

"I am very busy."

- "That is why I am calling you for an appointment.
Successful people are busy people. Sometimes you
can make more money by saving taxes than you can
by making more money. I think you will find the
ideas we discuss will be of interest and value to
you."

"I already give a lot to charity."

- "For that, all of society benefits and we thank you. I
want to meet with you to discuss some ideas that
are win-win. That means building a legacy that
benefits you while your legacy benefits society.
Whether you do anything or not, you will benefit
from learning about these ideas."

"I am not interested."

- "Let me assure you that I am not coming to ask for
a donation. I want to share some ideas with you that
might bear some fruit someday. I promise that you
will find these ideas to be of interest and of real
value."

Note: "No" does not mean no forever. Say this: "Things have
a way of changing. May I call you in 3-6 months to see if
anything has changed?" Few people ever follow up. You will
build credibility when you do. Keep following up every 3-6
months until the donor will finally meet with you.

So now you are in front of a wealthy potential donor, what do you do?

Explain that in addition to cash gifts and gifts of securities, there are other ways to benefit charities, build a legacy and enjoy benefits yourself. This is called charitable planned giving.

"Paying taxes is somewhat optional. There are ways to reduce taxes that we will discuss. How much you want to reduce your taxes is up to you. You may want to reduce the amount of income taxes you pay, or capital gains taxes or estate/gift taxes.

"What I am going to do is discuss several ideas that may be of interest to you. You will have to let me know which ones we should explore in more depth."

Go through the list of concepts outlined in the first section of this book and explain the tax savings inherent in each type of charitable tax planning vehicle. You may want to bring this book with you as a reference guide to explain the concepts and share examples of each.

The 3-5 Minute Presentation

Okay, so you have been given 3-5 minutes at a Board meeting, church service or other event. What are you going to say in that short time to create enough interest so someone will seek you out for more information?

Here is what we have done.

First, we would start with the importance of regular cash gifts to the charity's mission. Then explain that stocks can be gifted and avoid capital gains taxes. Life insurance policies with cash values can be gifted and avoid income taxes on any gains in the policy. Even land can be gifted under the right circumstances. Here is a script you can use:

"Life insurance can be used to create a large gift. Buy a policy and name the charity as owner and beneficiary. The premium will be tax deductible. You can use life insurance to leave a legacy gift such as a name on a building or branch. You can use a split dollar arrangement with your employer to buy a policy for charity and the employer will eventually recover all the funds advanced. Group life insurance in excess of $50,000 is taxable to the employee. You can gift the excess group life insurance to the charity and avoid taxes for this employee benefit.

"The biggest use of life insurance in charitable planned giving is to replace large charitable gifts. In this way, your heirs still inherit what they would have had you not made the gift to charity but now they get it income tax free, estate tax free and gift tax free. The donor benefits the charity and gets a large income tax deduction.

"Gift annuities can be used to guarantee a life income for the donors and benefit charity. The sale of an asset can be structured to minimize the taxes including the sale of a business.

"The Last Tithe in a will and trust guarantees that 10% of your estate when you both die will go to charity. It is your last opportunity to tithe.

"Charitable Remainder Trusts are split interest gifts to charity. The donors benefit from an income from the trust during their lifetimes. The charity gets the remainder of the trust after the donors' deaths. This can be used in the sale of an asset like stocks, real estate or business. It provides the donors with income tax deductions and avoidance of income or capital gains taxes upon the sale of the asset. It can be used as a deferred compensation vehicle.

"Charitable Lead Trusts provide a current benefit to charity and then after the designated time expires, the assets revert back to the donors or to the heirs of the donors.

"These and more ideas are available to those who want to save taxes and leave a legacy. To quote Ernest Becker, a Pulitzer Prize winner: **"What man fears most is not extinction but extinction with insignificance."**

"If any of what we shared has created some interest, please see me afterward or give me an email or call. I will be happy to explain more."

About the Author

James A Van Houten, CLU, ChFC, MSFS, MSM

Jim started in the financial services business in 1969. He is the second generation of Van Houtens to work in this industry. Jim is a retired General Agent for MassMutual Life. His agency encompassed Arizona and New Mexico. It was a very successful agency and earned numerous awards.

After retiring, Jim and his oldest son, Jameson, started Stonegate Financial Group as a SEC registered investment advisory firm. Jameson continues the business and has built it into one of the largest in Arizona. Jim retired from Stonegate in 2013.

Jim has a Bachelor of Science in Finance, Chartered Life Underwriter (CLU), Chartered Financial Consultant (ChFC), Master of Science in Financial Services (MSFS), and Master of Science in Management (MSM).

Asked to raise money for the YMCA in 1972, Jim did well and was then invited to join the Board of the Valley of the Sun YMCA. He served for 37 years and was its President in 1987. He also served on the National Board of the YMCA of the USA for 8 years.

Jim has raised many millions of dollars for charity through gift requests and planned giving plans.

He is a past Board member of the Barrows Neurological Institute Foundation, Arizona Friends of Foster Children Foundation, Claremont School of Theology, and Human Liberty ARTT Foundation. He is currently a member of the Advisory Board of the University of Arizona Cancer Center.

Jim has written numerous articles for national magazines and has spoken many times all over the country. This is his second book.

Jim and JeanneKay have been happily married for over 50 years. They have four sons, two daughters-in-law and five grandchildren.